What You Should Know About Your Conscience

... their conscience also bearing witness, and their thoughts the mean while accusing or else excusing one another (Romans 2.15).

NEVER HAS THE human race been so advanced in knowledge, and yet never have people been more confused about themselves and their mental make-up. Take the role of the conscience. What is this mysterious faculty? How does it function? And what happens when it is abused?

It is surprising that so little is heard about the conscience since it gives no end of trouble to practically everyone and is behind a lot of sickness and stress at the present time. There are many conditions of body as well as mind which physicians cannot get to the bottom of, and we can only guess at the problems inflicted by a suppressed conscience. It is said in the Bible that people may suffer debilitating and even fatal illnesses through the stifling of this faculty.[*] Great thinkers of the past saw the hand of conscience in life's strange afflictions to a degree seldom recognised today.

---

[*] *1 Corinthians 11.28-30.*

What is the conscience?

Among typical dictionary definitions of the conscience is the following: It is a faculty of self-awareness that judges our actions to see whether they are in harmony with our standards or beliefs.

King Solomon's definition, recorded in the *Book of Proverbs*, describes conscience as a kind of independent inspector within us. 'The spirit of man,' says Solomon, 'is the candle of the Lord, searching all the inward parts of the belly.' That is a most haunting and searching concept of the conscience. Solomon presents it as a faculty within us, attached to our minds, which operates on behalf of the Creator, sifting the inner motives behind the things we do, and laying bare our guilt.

The Greek word translated *conscience* in the New Testament literally means – *knowing together with*. It refers to an independent witness to our actions – like a personal ombudsman. The laws or standards of God are stamped on our constitution, and the faculty of conscience stands alongside, operating like a policeman or magistrate.

In many countries the judges are independent of state interference, and they jealously preserve that status. Other nations, however, do not have such a system, and they will sometimes say to a government that does, 'Why have you not told your judges to free that prominent subject of ours, whom you have charged with various crimes?' They seem to think that just as *they* overrule their judges, so all governments can do likewise. They are unable to grasp that others really do have an independent judiciary, and that the state cannot interfere. To a great extent, the conscience has this status. It certainly can be silenced, bent, manipulated and corrupted, but whatever we do, conscience always keeps a degree of independence, and it may at any time remember its original standards and produce sensations of shame and guilt. No matter how determined we may be to reprogramme the conscience, and conform it to what we want to think is right, it has a habit of recovering its independence. It is corruptible,

What You Should Know About Your
CONSCIENCE

PETER MASTERS

SWORD & TROWEL
METROPOLITAN TABERNACLE
LONDON

WHAT YOU SHOULD KNOW
ABOUT YOUR CONSCIENCE

© Peter Masters 1994
Fifth printing 2009

SWORD & TROWEL
Metropolitan Tabernacle
Elephant & Castle
London SE1 6SD

ISBN 978 1 899046 06 5

Cover design by Andrew Owen

All rights reserved. No part of this publication may be reproduced or transmitted in any form or by any means, electronic or mechanical, including photocopy, recording, or any information storage and retrieval system, without permission in writing from the publisher.

Printed by Harcourt Litho, Swansea, UK

yes, but never wholly corruptible. It will unexpectedly, and in various ways, assert its existence.

A troubled conscience may result in forms of mental anguish not readily connected with one's behaviour. A person may suddenly be overtaken by an unfathomable sense of unease, or of emptiness, purposelessness and despair. Someone may be plunged into deep depression (though a troubled conscience is by no means the only cause of depression, which may have an organic basis, or other causes). The prophet Isaiah warned of this when he uttered those famous words: 'The wicked are like the troubled sea, when it cannot rest, whose waters cast up mire and dirt. There is no peace, saith my God, to the wicked.'*

How is the conscience shaped?

But how can the conscience cause so much trouble? According to the atheistic view, it is only the product of childhood training. It is merely the *superego*, programmed by the views of parents and society. It is moulded by our environment, and therefore it should be possible for us to alter its moral values, and to train a new generation to accept updated standards.

This is the popular modern view of conscience, but it is not based on historic wisdom, and it has proved disastrously wrong. Countless people have shared their feelings of guilt with a counsellor only to be told that the problem is not what they have done, but the unreasonably high standard demanded by their conscience. They have been advised to reject this standard as unnecessary, and to learn a new and more lenient standard. Their counsellor has convinced them that they have the right to do whatever they want to do, as long as they do not injure anyone else in the process, and their conscience must get in line.

But, however much these counsellors attack the conscience as a

---

* *Isaiah 57.20-21.*

nuisance, and claim that it is retrainable, it refuses to submit fully and co-operate. Troubled people continue to suffer; depressed people continue to find no relief; and sufferers from mysterious, psychosomatic illnesses get no better.

After several decades of changing and conflicting theories from the 'anti-moral' wing of psychology, we should be ready to acknowledge that 'the foolishness of God is wiser than men.' In the Bible we are taught that the conscience is not shaped by human training or conditioning. Every conscience is primed by God. He embosses upon our human nature an awareness of His standards.

The apostle Paul shows that all people have a knowledge of right and wrong irrespective of their moral or cultural training. 'For there is no respect of persons with God,' he writes. 'For when the Gentiles, which have not the law *[non-Jewish nations, unfamiliar with Old Testament morality]*, do by nature the things contained in the law, these . . . shew the work of the law written in their hearts, their conscience also bearing witness.'[*]

Whether trained in moral and religious values or not, all people have God's moral code written within them, and no technique on earth can totally delete or change it. The conscience will rest contentedly when they operate in line with this moral code, and give great discomfort when they depart from it. People show how effective this conscience is by their reactions. When they offend, they find it necessary to ward off its pangs by justifying their actions and making excuses.

Where in the body is the conscience situated? If a pathologist wanted to locate it in a corpse, where would he find it? We cannot answer such questions. But the fact that it cannot be seen does not lead us to doubt its existence. We know it's there, because we have so often felt its operation. How often we have wished that we could force it to keep quiet about what we have done! If only we could have taken hold of it and brought it into line! How much shame, pain and

---

[*] *Romans 2.11, 14-15.*

unrest we would have avoided if only we could have switched it off, or transformed it into a source of reassurance! The conscience can certainly be anaesthetised or disabled by various techniques, but not entirely, or for ever.

The conscience remembers all

One of the great functions of the conscience, according to the Bible, is to bear witness to our wrongdoing on the day that we stand before God in judgement. Then, our conscience will testify against us. It will acknowledge all that we have done wrong, because it remembers![*] It keeps in mind the past history of our crimes, whether of thought, word or deed, and it may remind us of them at any time. When we finally stand before God, and all our guilty acts are paraded before us, it will be conscience that squirms and cries in response to each charge, 'I did that! I remember it!' That giant of literary genius John Bunyan, in his great allegory *The Holy War*, gives conscience the name of Mr Recorder. And so it is. It keeps a record.

In *John's Gospel* we read of an amazing occasion when the consciences of a group of proud Pharisees remembered their sins so vividly that they were completely overcome. Christ was teaching in the Temple when the scribes and Pharisees brought in a woman accused of adultery and asked Him whether she should be stoned, as commanded in the law of Moses. At first, He just stooped down and wrote on the ground as though He had not heard. But when they pressed Him, He said, 'He that is without sin among you, let him first cast a stone at her.' And suddenly, they were so convicted by their consciences, that they left 'one by one, beginning at the eldest, even unto the last.'

Though they were religious leaders, they were hypocrites, guilty of adulterous acts themselves. When challenged, their consciences (though long suppressed) howled within them, and they were

---

[*] *Romans 2.15-16.*

compelled to slink away and be publicly humiliated. Conscience is capable of snatching away the self-confidence and poise of the proudest person even years after the sin was committed. It has a long memory.

Conscience will eventually stir

In Bunyan's *Holy War*, Mr Recorder so disturbed the people of the town of Mansoul by his crying out against their crimes that they seized him and locked him up in a dungeon to silence him. But every so often he managed to break free, and would roar out with such vehemence that his voice shook the whole town. You can suppress conscience, and you can run away from it, but after a while it may speak again, and sometimes with a mighty voice which nothing will silence.

This is illustrated by the experience of an American woman whose crisis of conscience drew international publicity. From being a student-protest organiser in the 1960s, she graduated to terrorism in 1970. To secure funds for the arming of the Black Panthers, she plotted with others to rob a bank, but the bank raid went wrong, and a policeman was shot. Several offenders were caught and convicted, but this woman got away. She changed her identity, and moved to another part of the country, and, although she became the object of the largest woman-hunt in FBI history, she remained undetected. Eventually the case was closed and 23 years afterwards there remained little chance that she would ever be linked with that long-forgotten incident.

But then conscience stirred, and suddenly this woman, by now middle-aged and respectable, could no longer live with her crime. When the pain became unbearable she made her way into a hospital evening class on depression. Her instructor recalled: 'I've never seen anybody in such psychic pain.' She gave herself up, ready to face life imprisonment or even death rather than live with that pain. Conscience had broken free from its dungeon and roared out, and this poor woman could no longer live in peace. Cases of this kind – and they are innumerable – can only be accounted for by the existence of the conscience. Why otherwise would people be driven to confess – to their pain and loss – when they are safely beyond discovery?

The long memory of the conscience is also seen in the case of a once highly popular musical performer and quiz show host. Having made his fortune from broadcasting and record sales, and at the height of his fame, he was plunged into depression about his boyhood misdemeanours. As a teenager, apparently, he had stolen from the open counters of a well-known chain store, and though for years it did not trouble him, suddenly it all came back. Success, fame, admirers, money, luxuries, and every kind of pleasure, could not soothe his aching conscience once it began to speak. Eventually, when he could take it no more, he hit on the idea of writing an article in a national tabloid, confessing in detail what he had done. He would reveal all, and so purge his agonised conscience.

Such remedies, however, are generally doomed to long-term failure, for there is only one way to purge and calm an inflamed and throbbing conscience. Only the Lord Who gave the conscience can relieve it, as we shall see in due course.

The apostle Paul was once under arrest in the garrison of the Roman procurator of Judea, Governor Felix, a cunning and violent individual who had proved utterly remorseless throughout his climb to power. But when Paul challenged him about his soul, his insensible conscience burst into life, and in full view of his officers his body trembled and shook with fear. That silent conscience had not, after all, ceased to function!

Not long before the writing of this booklet, a large and delightful old house in a northern English town was modernised by builders. Under the floorboards they found a suicide note dated August 1901. The owner of the property had murdered his maid some years before, and had escaped suspicion. But with the passing of time he could no longer stand the burden of conscience, and took his life, leaving a full confession. How many people have found the outraged conscience to be more than they could bear?

If conscience can make people willing to court shame and public humiliation, or to face prison and the death sentence, or to take their own lives, is it not obvious that it can provoke other manifestations of pain and unrest in our lives? Of course it can! The conscience is powerful and implacable once aroused. We abuse it at our peril.

Because the conscience can be silenced for long periods, many people think that its memory has been blotted out, but this is a great mistake. A leading drug baron made a similar miscalculation, to the delight of the British police, when he committed all his criminal arrangements and deals to a portable notebook-computer, thinking that everything could be erased when he chose. For several years frustrated investigators had failed to secure evidence against this sophisticated crook. They knew so much about his operations, but no hard evidence ever materialised. Then his discarded and 'erased' notebook-computer fell into their hands, and experts were able to retrieve the information supposedly wiped off.

Smart as he was, this crime boss had not known that he could not completely eradicate that information, and that a laboratory could recover it from the depths of the device. The result was a major success for the police, and the humbling of a seemingly invincible drug trafficker. Conscience, also, can never be erased, nor can you buy its silence for ever.

Methods of silencing the conscience
(i) 'Steamrollering'

People try four main ways of silencing conscience and avoiding its pangs. The most common of these is to steamroller it down by repeated sins of thought, word and deed. The conscience may be silenced by simply burying it in misdemeanours, and ignoring it. Like a teacher who gradually becomes hoarse and then speechless in a rioting class, so the conscience is silenced as we grow used to our wrongdoing. The first sin hurts, the next a little less, and so on, until we feel no qualms at all. This technique, though, does not work well for everyone, nor for every kind of sin. And for many people the conscience keeps waking up.

(ii) Self-justifying arguments

A second way of silencing conscience is to argue with it whenever it objects to anything that you do. Shout it down. Justify what you have done, and complain to your conscience just as an angry teenager may round on a parent. Tell your conscience that it wasn't your fault, that it is being unreasonable, and that no one else does things that way. Boast of your imagined virtues, and tell conscience to keep out of your affairs. This bullish approach works fairly well for many people, but it has the disadvantage of creating resentment in the conscience – a problem we will refer to again.

(iii) Diversionary tactics

Another technique for avoiding pangs of conscience is that of diverting your thoughts every time the conscience speaks. This is difficult to do if conscience wakes you in the night when you lie helpless in bed. But for waking hours this is the method chosen by many. They rush for the television, or to music or some other form of entertainment. This is much easier to do now than it was years ago. If you need to get away from your thoughts you can easily drown them by clapping on a set of headphones.

Some people, when conscience begins to murmur, divert their thoughts to their responsibilities, even to trials and problems (as long as these do not remind them of their sins), or to plans, house decorations or holidays. Anything will do if it smothers and silences the unwanted voice of conscience. Some people defend themselves by going on the offensive against the sins of someone else. In the fury of their campaign or war, they can forget their own faults and even feel self-righteous.

Many opt for friendly, talkative company, and some escape into drink or drugs. The trouble, though, with any diversionary technique, is that you cannot run for ever. And as you get older, and your mental legs get slower, conscience catches up.

(iv) Reprogramming the conscience

We have already mentioned the technique of reprogramming the conscience, and this is certainly the most elaborate way of trying to secure peace and quiet. To succeed (but you can never totally succeed) you must convince yourself that all morality is unreasonable nonsense invented by prudes and hypocrites who are out to destroy the enjoyment of life. Ideally, you need to adopt atheism. You must read the literature of atheism, and talk with people who can persuade you that it's true. You must convince yourself that there is no God, no day of judgement, and no afterlife. This is the foundation you will need in order to change and rebuild your entire value system and scheme of moral standards.

Many people go this way, hoping that their conscience will be silenced, and they will be able to do whatever they like without the slightest shame or regret. They even try to maximise their comfort by persuading society around to think the same way, and they want the next generation brought up to believe that adultery is reasonable, homosexuality is a valid lifestyle, and so on.

What are your chances of success? You may appear to achieve your objective. You may reach the point where deeds which once made you feel ashamed no longer bother you. But this will not be the end of the story. If you get to the point where your conscience is successfully neutered, you will find yourself to be 'out-of-sorts' as a person. You will be a walking contradiction. You will be a person with feet pointing in different directions. You will have tampered with your conscience and twisted your natural constitution to accept an immoral set of standards. But you are more complex than you think, and you will now be a deeply troubled man or woman, a divided person, because you cannot get rid of the original programme of conscience.

In reality, your conscience will be like a poor, battered child. A vicious parent smacks the child across the mouth in an attempt to silence him. As the child whimpers in pain, the parent lashes out again and again, punching and bruising the pathetic victim into terrified submission. Now the child dares not murmur, and chokes back every sob. But bitterness and resentment contorts that battered little face, and one day it will be expressed. He is sullen and silent for now, but he will not forget.

The revenge of the conscience

The person who bludgeons the conscience into submission has a world of pent-up agony within, and a price yet to pay, for the conscience is a living thing and it cannot be abused without consequences. It may be scared to tell you what it thinks of you, but it will look at you, from within, with contempt in its eyes, and one day it will inflict upon you a wretchedness that words will not be able to express. The silenced conscience will have its revenge.

Many years ago I knew a young university professor whose accomplishments in a particular field of scholarship were considerable. Naturally, he had access to the leading academic libraries, and from one of these he stole a rare and valuable book. Because he could not eradicate the large, ornate stamp of the library, he obliterated it by sticking his own coloured, printed label over the top.

A few years later, he lent this book to an academic friend, proud that he could appear to own such a work. But, unfortunately for him, he had not noticed what had happened to the label. Somehow, his own label had absorbed the ink of the underlying stamp, so that the library's claim to ownership showed clearly through. It was only after the book was returned to him that he saw for himself the effects of time, and realised to his horror that his friend would know he was a thief. He felt utterly embarrassed and ashamed. What could he do? What could he say? How could he ever explain this?

I cannot now relate the outcome of this story, but the conscience behaves like the underlying stamp in that book. You may stick what you like over it – even new moral standards – but in the end the old rules will show through. Your conscience will never entirely stop reading its God-given values, and this will unsettle you in ways you will not understand.

For as long as new information is pasted across your conscience, you will be a troubled and divided person. Your inner lack of peace may lead to a broken marriage, or to a crazy degree of workaholism, or to alcoholism, or to any number of other troubles or escapist excesses. It may lead to the level of personal unease that unleashes temper tantrums, physical violence, harrowing depression, or the kind of psychosomatic illnesses we have already mentioned. When a vessel's wheelhouse is disabled, there is no knowing whether it will capsize slowly in heavy seas, or suddenly on rocks or quicksands.

The Bible refers to people who speak lies in hypocrisy and have their consciences seared with a hot iron. They have become such inveterate liars that conscience is cauterised and sealed off. It is as though they have carried out some kind of operation on themselves to close it up, so that it cannot function at all. But though it cannot speak, it can still hurt, and it can still record and remember sin in readiness for the day of judgement.

It is very noticeable that people who turn themselves into militant atheists to stifle their consciences, become extremely aggressive when talking about morals or religion. Does this not betray the fact that it is a constant fight to keep the conscience buttoned up? This kind of anger saturates atheistic periodicals, in which columnists become worked up to such a pitch of abusiveness against religious faith, it is clear that there is a world of contradiction within them.

How conscience affects character

Apart from the self-inflicted psychological trauma sustained by a person who has silenced or reprogrammed the conscience, there are other consequences. It is obvious that such a person is likely to become increasingly unrestrained in the pursuit of whims and lusts. Human beings need a functioning conscience to hold them in check. Without this, they constantly grow more lawless and arrogant. There is no knowing the extremes to which we may go either in secret perversion or open wickedness once the conscience is disabled. It is a priceless and indispensable benefit to us.

Also, the disabling or anaesthetising of the conscience tears away one of the greatest comforts of life. Conscience, after all, is not just a faculty of warning. It is also very reassuring. It not only speaks out against wrong, but provides a sense of approval and peace when our conduct is right.

If you suppress and gag the conscience you immediately become an insecure person. Outwardly, you may appear confident, but inwardly you do not know where you are any more. You do not know the worth of what you are doing; whether it is right or wrong. You have no awareness of what is really fair. You have no basis of judgement for any of the deep decisions of life, and you will join the ranks of those who have no anchorage and peace in the storms of life. Your conscience, when respected, tells you what is fair or reasonable, and you can trust it. Rightly used and honoured, it enables you to have a fixed point of reference for all your thinking.

Relief of the burdened conscience

The final portion of this brief look at the conscience must focus on the subject of how it may be unburdened. Many people want to suppress their consciences because they cannot stand the aching shame which lingers from *past* deeds. Because there is a market for the relief of burdened consciences, the world offers many products, all at a price. Some religions offer penances and special rituals, but what can these possibly do to ease away guilt? We have noted how some psychological therapists question the *values* with which conscience is impregnated, and try to persuade their clients to switch them for others. But such therapy always fails sooner or later.

There is only one way of easing the troubled conscience, and that is by obtaining forgiveness from the Lord of the conscience. The Bible insists that the conscience must be purged by the blood of Christ.[*]

If you were to owe a large sum of money, and this debt kept you awake at night and robbed you of all peace and enjoyment, nothing would ease your mind other than the settling of the debt. But this debt you cannot pay, and you can see no way how it can be paid. What if you discovered, however, that a friend had heard of your problem, and paid the debt? The power of that debt to enslave you in worry would then be broken. Its claims and demands would have been fully met.

The conscience, similarly, can be at peace only when its claims and charges are met, and its debts paid. It tells me that I have sinned against God. It points out all my pride, selfishness, dishonesty, greed, unbelief, meanness, hostility, and so many other things besides. I have hated it for that. But now I want peace. How can I satisfy conscience? How can I escape the guilt and remorse of all that I have done in my life? Only by knowing that Jesus Christ, the Second Person in the glorious Godhead, has come into the world to take the punishment due to me for my sin. He came to die in the place of all those who seek His forgiveness.

If I am among those who trust in Christ, and seek Him, then I can be sure that He died for me also. For me He suffered indescribable agony on the cross of Calvary, bore away my sin, purchasing the right to forgive me and make me His child. He has paid my debt, and paid it fully. What can purge the conscience? Only the forgiveness of God, secured by the atoning death of the Lord Jesus Christ. He is our sin-bearer. The blood of Christ (says the letter to the *Hebrews*) shall 'purge your conscience . . . to serve the living God.'

It is most interesting to note that the Greek word translated 'purge' in that Scripture text is a word which we use today in the English

---

[*] *Hebrews 9.14.*

language. We use this Greek term *catharsis* to describe a dramatic release of emotion which supposedly relieves grief or fear or other great tensions. It describes an emotional event, usually deliberately worked up, intended to purge out the emotional system, and get rid of something which is psychologically troubling.

Though now an increasingly discredited form of therapy, some psychologists still claim that beneficial results can occur. A *catharsis* is achieved by methods such as the sharing of sensitive, intimate, personal matters. In the highly charged and tense moment of self-revelation (abreaction), there may be such a release of emotion that the troublesome fear (or whatever it may be) might seem to be purged out, and a special bond of trust and understanding established with the therapist.

There is no doubt that the disclosure of highly personal and potentially embarrassing confidences does produce a deep emotional experience, which many people have learned to exploit. But this can no more heal or change the inner person than the gushing of water from an over-fierce hot shower.

As far as the human heart is concerned, the only true *catharsis* or purging is the one mentioned in the Bible. This is the glorious relief and cleansing which comes when we believe that Christ's death has cancelled all the charges of sin which stand against us. Wesley sings:

> *He breaks the power of cancelled sin,*
> *He sets the prisoner free;*
> *His blood can make the foulest clean;*
> *His blood availed for me.*

When we know that God has forgiven us, then the conscience is at rest. If we are far away from God, and have never thought about these things, our greatest need is to bring all our sin to Him, and to ask Him to forgive us. If we are sincere, He will throw our mountain of sin into the sea of His forgetfulness, where it will never be remembered or held against us. We must trust only in what Christ the Saviour has done in suffering on the cross to pay the penalty of our sin. And we must give our lives wholly to Him. Then shall the conscience be purged and at rest, and we shall have fellowship with God, and His Son, Jesus Christ.

The forgiveness of Almighty God is the most amazing benefit that can be imagined. Why should God forgive us? We do not deserve anything from Him. Why should Christ have come from Heaven to earth to die in indescribable agony for us? Words such as grace, lovingkindness, compassion and mercy are not enough to convey the immensity of the love of God in providing for us, and saving us from our sin.

Conscience – the last word

What could be worse than to end life's journey a stranger to this mercy? What could be more foolish than to come to the close of this brief, earthly existence, having missed the point of it all? One day, for each of us, the light of this world must snap out, and the light of the next be turned on. Will it be a day of great gladness, on which we embark upon the greatest experience for a human soul, that of soaring into eternity and into the presence of God, filled with an irrepressible sense of anticipation and glory?

Or will it be a day of terror, when your conscience, the lifelong witness to your deeds, and partner of your cares, will remember the wounds of a lifetime in your service, and shriek out in final anger – 'What have you done to us? Where have you brought us? I tried to tell you when you went wrong! You would never listen! You ignored my every cry! Now it is too late. O, how I warned you! I warned you!'

You have a conscience. Think about the implications of this. Think what it points to – your Creator and His standards, and your accountability. Think also about your greatest needs – the forgiveness of the Lord, and the new and spiritual life that comes with it. And go personally in prayer to the God Who is ready to forgive those who throw themselves upon His mercy.

Other booklets by Dr Peter Masters

The Rebellious Years
Subtitled *The Need for Self-Understanding*. This booklet is intended to help readers from mid-teenage to late twenties to understand the source of the inner rebellion that urges us all away from God in the 'second quarter' of life.

How to Seek and Find the Lord
Intended for seekers, the author emphasises that there is only one way of salvation, clearly defined and revealed by God in His Word. He then explains the kind of belief and attitude which brings a seeker to find the Lord.

Vanity of Vanities
Subtitled *The Emptiness of Life Without God*. This booklet presents the experience of King Solomon, who experimented with every conceivable kind of pleasure, and concluded that life is pointless and predictable, unless people seek and find the Lord God, and know His power and guidance in their lives.

A Seeker's Problems
Often when people are convinced of the need for conversion to Christ they experience difficulty in seeking and finding Him as Saviour. This booklet answers ten problems encountered by serious seekers. These are not questions or doubts about the faith, but personal hindrances in approaching Christ, by faith. Many seekers have been helped by the advice given here.

Available from: Tabernacle Bookshop, Metropolitan Tabernacle, Elephant & Castle, London SE1 6SD   www.TabernacleBookshop.org

Audio and video sermons of Dr Masters
are available free on the Metropolitan Tabernacle's website:
www.MetropolitanTabernacle.org

Two illustrated paperback volumes of Christian biography, presenting the lives and conversion to God of 25 famous, unusual or even notorious people, including royals, Reformers, and 'fathers' of modern science.

Men of Destiny
Peter Masters

166 pages, paperback, Wakeman Trust, ISBN 978 1 870855 55 6

Tsar Alexander Pavlovich *(The tsar who defeated Napoleon)*
Lieut 'Birdie' Bowers *(Scott's 'bravest man' in the Antarctic)*
Sir James Simpson *(The discoverer of anaesthetic chloroform)*
Alves Reis *(The counterfeiter who nearly owned his country)*
Joshua Poole *(The story of 'Fiddler Joss', drunkard turned preacher)*
Viscount Alexander of Hillsborough *(A leader of the House of Lords)*
John Newton *(The transformed slave-trader)*
Jean Henri Dunant *(Founder of the International Red Cross)*
Martin Luther *(The ex-monk who led the Reformation)*
Bilney, Tyndale & Latimer *(Three heroic English martyrs)*
Alfred the Great *(The king who organised England)*
Lieut-General Sir William Dobbie *(World War II hero of Malta)*

Men of Purpose
Peter Masters

157 pages, paperback, Wakeman Trust, ISBN 978 1 870855 41 9

Michael Faraday *(Father of electrical science)*
Henry J. Heinz *(Founder of the food empire)*
Felix Mendelssohn *(A composer with a spiritual journey)*
Lord Radstock *(Whose missions brought conversions to Russia's aristocracy)*
James Clerk Maxwell *(Father of modern physics)*
Philip P. Bliss *(The hymnwriter who won countless souls)*
Fred Charrington *(The brewer who renounced a fortune)*
Lord Kelvin *(Britain's greatest scientific inventor)*
James Montgomery *(A poet who ran away from God)*
Sir John Ambrose Fleming *(Inventor of the radio valve)*
Daniel Defoe *(The founder of journalism and great novelist)*

These books are available from Christian bookshops, and from:
Tabernacle Bookshop, Metropolitan Tabernacle, Elephant & Castle,
London SE1 6SD   www.TabernacleBookshop.org